OUTSIDE
THE DREAM

OUTSIDE THE DREAM

CHILD POVERTY IN AMERICA

PHOTOGRAPHS BY STEPHEN SHAMES

INTRODUCTION BY JONATHAN KOZOL
AFTERWORD BY MARIAN WRIGHT EDELMAN

APERTURE

CHILDREN'S DEFENSE FUND

"The problem of the children becomes perplexing. Their very number makes one stand aghast....For be it remembered, these children with the training they receive—or do not receive—with the instincts they inherit and absorb in their growing up, are to be our future rulers, if our theory of government is worth anything."

JACOB RIIS

IMMOKOLEE, FLORIDA, 1985

America is a dream. We are a nation created by our collective dreams. Our founding fathers dreamed of "life, liberty, and the pursuit of happiness." My grandparents came to this country to fulfill their dream of religious freedom. Martin Luther King, Jr. had a dream of freedom. Others dreamt of material success, a better life. Millions continue migrating to our shores with their dreams and aspirations because America continues to be the place where dreams come true.

Yet within our borders a generation of American children exists outside the dream. They have been left behind in poverty and despair. It is as if they are not part of this great country, not part of the American dream. There are more than 12 million American children living in poverty. They constitute more than one-third of all poor people in America. Today, the poor are children. And their numbers are growing.

I met many children on my travels. I talked with "babies" who had babies themselves. I photographed the offspring of the "working poor" and the unemployed. I looked through the camera at youth in urban ghettos. I lived with homeless kids in parks and beaches. I observed college-bound teenagers studying by a lantern and siblings protecting and parenting each other. I documented youngsters coping with social problems, unexpected emergencies, and just plain bad luck. I witnessed stress, violence, and frustration; but also love, hope, and extraordinary courage.

It is never easy seeing pain. It made me feel sad and often powerless to witness the self-destructive and dangerous acts thousands of our young people commit every day. These were hard to photograph, as they must be difficult for you to view in this book. But we must look and see. We cannot ignore the plight of one-fifth of our heirs if we are to stop the destruction of a generation of children.

The youths pictured here, like those in the famous Farm Security Administration photographs from the Great Depression, will continue to be remembered for years to come. And like their 1930s counterparts, history may decide to view them as heroic. These are good kids. They are likeable. They have dreams and hopes. Perhaps this book will help us allow these children to become part of the American dream.

STEPHEN SHAMES

TO JOSHUA

INTRODUCTION BY JONATHAN KOZOL

On an average morning in Chicago, about 5,700 children in 190 classrooms come to school only to find they have no teacher. Victimized by endemic funding shortages, the system can't afford sufficient substitutes to take the place of missing teachers. "We've been in this typing class a whole semester," says a 15-year-old at Du Sable High, "and they still can't find us a teacher."

In a class of 39 children at Chicago's Goudy Elementary School, an adult is screaming at a child: "Keisha, look at me... Look me in the eye!" Keisha is fighting with a classmate. Over what? It turns out: over a crayon, said the *Chicago Tribune*, in 1988. Last January the underfunded school began rationing supplies.

The odds these black kids in Chicago face are only slightly worse than those faced by low-income children all over America. Children like these will be the parents of the year 2000. Many of them will be unable to earn a living and fulfill adult obligations; they will see their families disintegrate, their children lost to drugs and destitution. When we later condemn them for "parental failings," as we inevitably will do, we may be forced to stop and remember how we also failed them in the first years of their lives.

It is commonplace that a society reveals its reverence or contempt for history by the respect or disregard that it displays for older people. The way we treat our children tells us something of the future we envision. The willingness of the nation to relegate so many of these poorly housed, poorly fed, and poorly educated children to the role of outcasts in a rich society is going to come back to haunt us.

With nearly 15 percent of high-school students dropping out before they graduate it is not surprising that illiteracy figures continue to worsen. The much publicized volunteer literacy movement promoted for the last six years by Barbara Bush serves only 200,000 of the nation's millions of functional illiterates. Meanwhile, the gulf in income between rich and poor American families is wider than at any time since figures were recorded, starting in the 1940s. The richest 20 percent receive 44.6 percent of national family income; the poorest 20 percent got only 4.6 percent. Almost 5 million of the poorest group are children.

Disparities in wealth play out in financing of schools. Low-income children, who receive the least at home, receive the least from public education. New Trier High School, for example, serving children from such affluent suburbs as Winnetka, Illinois, pays its better teachers 50 percent above the highest paid teachers at Du Sable, by no means the worst school in Chicago. The public schools in affluent Great Neck and White Plains, New York, spend twice as much per pupil as the schools that serve the children of the Bronx.

Infant mortality figures are classic indices of health in most societies. The gap between white and black infant mortality continues to widen, reaching a 47-year high in 1987 (the most recent year for which data are available). Black children are more than twice as likely to die in infancy as whites—nine times as likely to be neurologically impaired. One possible consequence: black children are almost three times as likely as whites to be identified as mentally retarded by their public schools.

Federal programs initiated in the 1960s to assist low-income children, though far from universally successful, made solid gains in preschool education (Head Start), compensatory reading (Chapter 1), and pre-college preparation (Upward Bound), while sharply cutting the rates of infant death and child malnutrition. Limited funding, however, narrowed the scope of all these efforts. Head Start, for example, never has reached more than one of five low-income children between its start-up in the '60s and today.

Rather than expand these programs, President Reagan kept them frozen or else cut them to the bone. In 1989, living stipends paid to welfare families with children were 37 percent (adjusted for inflation) below the 1970 level. Nearly half a million families lost all welfare payments. In the early 1980s, a million people were cut from food stamps; 2 million kids were dropped from school-lunch programs. The WIC program (Women, Infants, Children), which provides emergency nutrition supplements to low-income infants, young children, and pregnant women, was another target of Reagan administration cuts, but Congress successfully fought them off. Despite its efforts, the WIC budget is woefully inadequate, and provides services to less than 60 percent of the children and women who meet the eligibility requirements.

Federal housing funds were also slashed during these years. As these cutbacks took their tolls, homeless children were seen begging in the streets of major cities for the first time since the Great Depression. In 1986 alone, a fivefold increase in homeless children was seen in Washington, D.C. By 1987 nearly half the occupants of homeless shelters in New York City were children. The average homeless child was only six years old.

The lives of homeless children tell us much about the disregard that society has shown for vulnerable people. Many of these kids grow up surrounded by diseases no longer seen in most developed nations. Whooping cough and tuberculosis, once regarded as archaic illnesses, are now familiar in the shelters. Shocking numbers of these children have not been inoculated and for this reason cannot go to school. Those who do attend school may be two years behind grade level.

Many get to class so tired and hungry that they cannot concentrate. Others are ashamed to go to school because of shunning by their peers. Classmates label them "the hotel children" and don't want to sit beside them. Even their teachers sometimes keep their distance. The children look diseased and dirty. Many times they are. Often unable to bathe, they bring the smell of destitution with them into school. There *is* a smell of destitution, I may add. It is the smell of sweat and filth and urine.

Continued on next page

Eleanor was 14, a child herself, when she gave birth to Livita (who is eight months old in this photo). Seven children, including Eleanor and her daughter, live with Eleanor's mother in a two-room tenament on Chicago's gang-ridden West Side. Less than a year after Livita was born Eleanor became pregnant again.

CHICAGO, ILLINOIS, 1985

Like many journalists, I often find myself ashamed to be resisting the affection of a tiny child whose entire being seems to emanate pathology.

So, in a terrifying sense, these children have become American untouchables. Far from demonstrating more compassion, administration leaders have resorted to a stylized severity in speaking of poor children. Children denied the opportunity for Head Start, sometimes health care, housing, even certified schoolteachers, have nevertheless been told by William J. Bennett, preaching from his bully pulpit as U.S. Secretary of Education under Reagan, that they would be held henceforth to "higher standards." Their parents—themselves too frequently the products of dysfunctional and underfunded urban schools—have nonetheless been lectured on their "lack of values." Efforts begun more than 10 years ago to equalize school funding between districts have been put on the back burner and are now replaced by strident exhortations to the poor to summon "higher motivation" and, no matter how debilitated by disease or hunger, to "stand tall." Celebrities are hired to sell children on the wisdom of not dropping out of school. The White House tells them they should "just say no" to the temptations of the streets. But hope cannot be marketed as easily as blue jeans. Certain realities—race and class and caste—are there and they remain.

What is the consequence of tougher rhetoric and more severe demands? Higher standards, in the absence of authentic educative opportunities in early years, function as a punitive attack on those who have been cheated since their infancy. Effectively, we now ask more of those to whom we now give less. Earlier testing for school children is prescribed. Those who fail are penalized by being held back from promotion and by being slotted into lower tracks where they cannot impede the progress of more privileged children. Those who disrupt classroom discipline are not placed in smaller classes with more patient teachers; instead, at a certain point, they are expelled—even if this means expulsion of a quarter of all pupils in the school. The pedagogic hero of the Reagan White House was Joe Clark—a principal who roamed the hallways of his segregated high school in New Jersey with a bullhorn and a bat and managed to raise reading scores by throwing out his low-achieving pupils.

In order to justify its abdication, the federal government has called for private business to assist the underfunded urban schools. While business leaders have responded with some money, they also have brought a very special set of values and priorities. The primary concern of business is the future productivity of citizens. Education is regarded as capital investment. The child is seen as raw material that needs a certain processing before it is of value. The question posed, therefore, is how much money it is worth investing in a certain child to obtain a certain economic gain. Educators, eager to win corporate support, tell business leaders what they want to hear. "We must start thinking of students as workers," says the head of the American Federation of Teachers, Albert Shanker.

The notion of kids as workers raises an unprecedented question. Is future productivity the only rationale for their existence? A lot of the things that make existence wonderful are locked out of the lives of children seen primarily as future clerical assistants or as possible recruits to office pools at IBM. The other consequence of "productivity" thinking is an increased willingness to make predictions about children based almost entirely on their social status. Those whose present station seems to promise most are given most. Those whose origins are least auspicious are provided with stripped-down education. IQ testing of low-income babies has been recently proposed in order to identify those who are particularly intelligent and to accord them greater educational advantages, although this means that other babies will be stigmatized by their exclusion.

A heightened discrimination in the use of language points to a dual vision: we speak of the need to "train" the poor, but "educate" the children of the middle class and rich. References to "different learning styles" and the need to "target" different children with "appropriate" curricula are now becoming fashionable ways of justifying stratified approaches. Early tracking is one grim result. A virtual retreat from any efforts at desegregation is another: if children of different social classes need "appropriate" and "different" offerings, it is more efficient and sensible to teach them separately.

A century ago, Lord Acton spoke thus of the United States: "In a country where there is no distinction of class, a child is not born to the station of its parents, but with an indefinite claim to all the prizes that can be won by thought and labor. It is in conformity with the theory of equality... to give as near as possible to every youth an equal start in life." Americans, he said, "are unwilling that any should be deprived in childhood of the means of competition."

That this tradition has been utterly betrayed in recent years is now self-evident. The sense of fairness, however, runs deep in the thinking of Americans. Though frequently eclipsed, it is a theme that stubbornly recurs. A quarter century ago, it took disruptions in the streets to force Americans to question the unfairness of de jure segregation. Today it is not law but economics that condemns the children of the very poor to the implacable inheritance of a diminished destiny. "No matter what they do," says the superintendent of Chicago's public schools, "their lot has been determined."

Between the dream and the reality there falls the shadow of the ghetto school, the ghetto hospital, the homeless shelter. Appeals to the pocketbook have done no good. Black leaders have begun to contemplate the need for massive protests by poor people. Middle-class students, viscerally shocked by the hard edge of poverty they see in city streets, may be disposed to join them. The price may be another decade of societal disruption. The reward may be the possibility that we can enter the next century not as two nations, vividly unequal, but as the truly democratic nation we profess to be and have the power to become. Whether enough people think this outcome worth the price, however, is by no means clear.❏

Kevin, 11, sleeps in the front seat of the family car. A 13-year-old brother makes his bed in the back seat. "This is not an easy life for the kids," says their mother. "My children have changed schools three times. Their classmates call them hobos."

Ventura, California, 1985

Though Ricky and Mary's mother works full time as a short-order cook, they're still poor.

CLEWISTON, FLORIDA, 1985

Oscar uses the fourth floor fire escape of the Holland Hotel as a jungle gym. Located in Times Square, the hotel—which warehouses hundreds of homeless families at a cost of more than $1000 per month, per family—does not have a community room or supervised activities.

NEW YORK CITY, 1987

BRONX, NEW YORK, 1989

*E*very day
27 American
children die
from the effects
of poverty.

BROOKLYN, NEW YORK, 1988

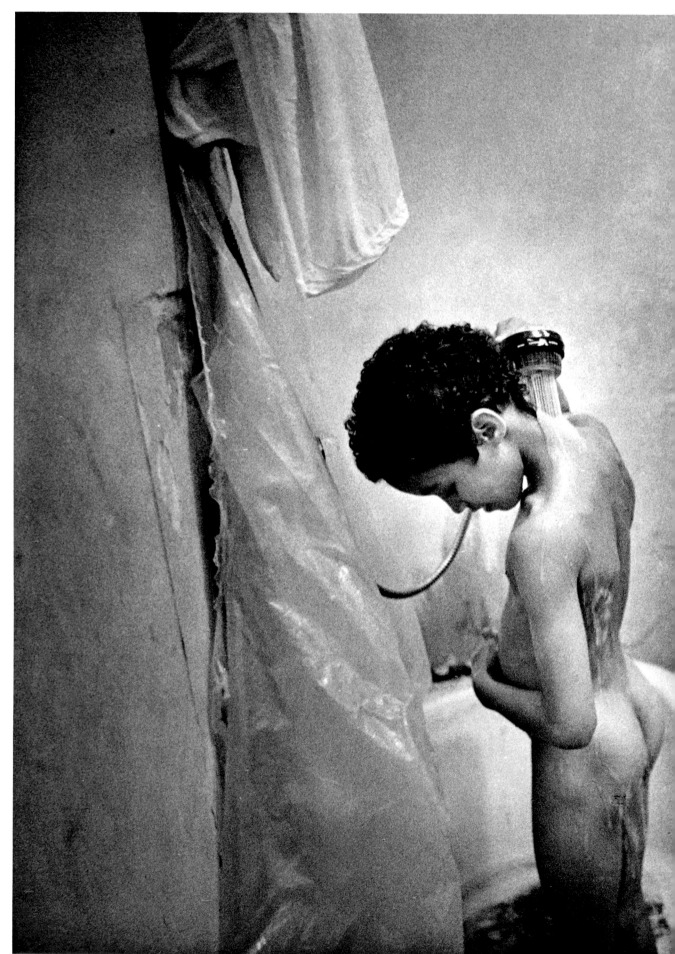

BRONX, NEW YORK, 1989

CHICAGO, ILLINOIS, 1985

Every day more than 12 million children wake up poor.

ORANGE COUNTY, CALIFORNIA, 1984

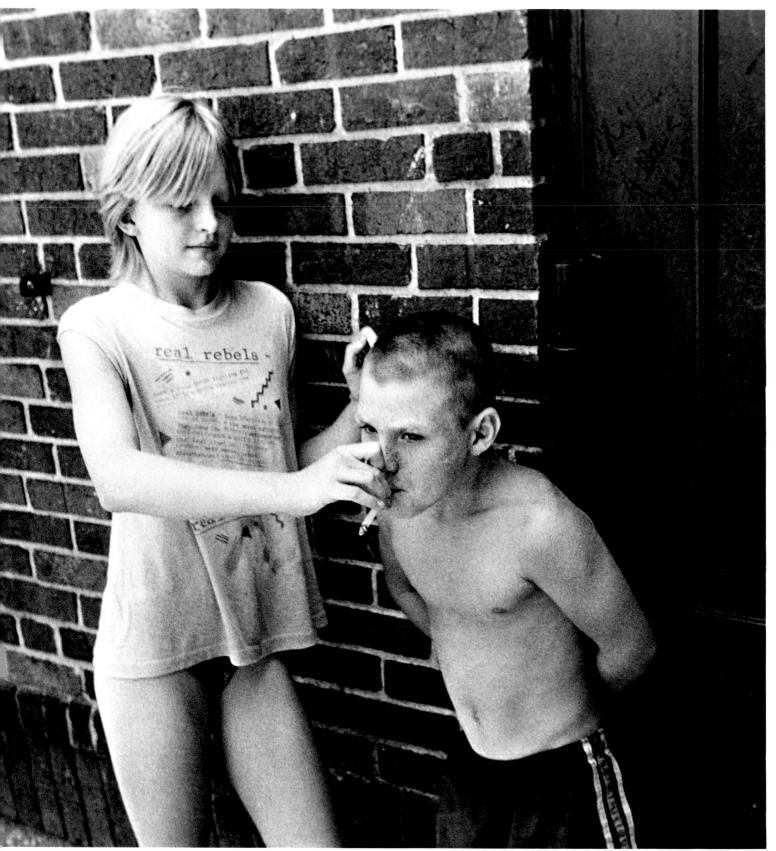

CINCINNATI, OHIO, 1985

ORANGE COUNTY, CALIFORNIA, 1984

*E*very day
135,000 children
bring guns to
school. Every day
10 children die
from guns, and 30
are wounded.

ORANGE COUNTY, CALIFORNIA, 1984

Every day 100,000 American children are homeless. In fact, one-third of homeless shelter residents are children and their families.

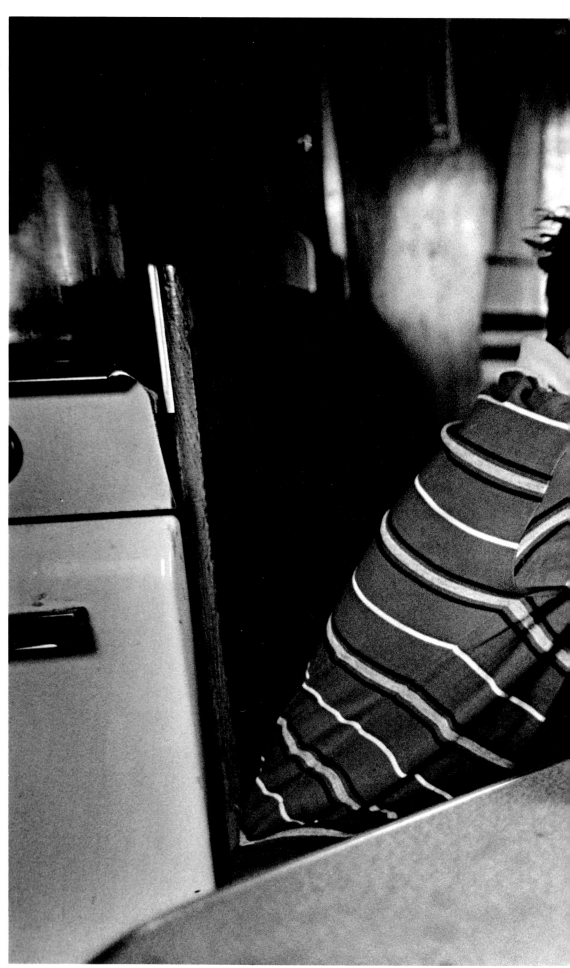

VENTURA, CALIFORNIA, 1985

Ventura, California, 1985

Bob, his wife, sister, and five children live in a 6-by-13 foot trailer on the beach at McGrath State Park in Ventura County. The trailer was purchased with a no-interest loan from a local church group. Twelve families and their 35 children live in the park more or less permanently. Getting their children to school regularly was a major problem for all the families. It took a year to convince the local school board to have the school bus stop at McGrath. Top left: Doris worked as a nurse until February 1984, when a drunk driver hit her car and she became disabled. Without her income, the family—Doris, her husband Mike, and their daughter Cathy—lost their home.

CINCINNATI, OHIO, 1985

BRONX, NEW YORK, 1977

BRONX, NEW YORK, 1981

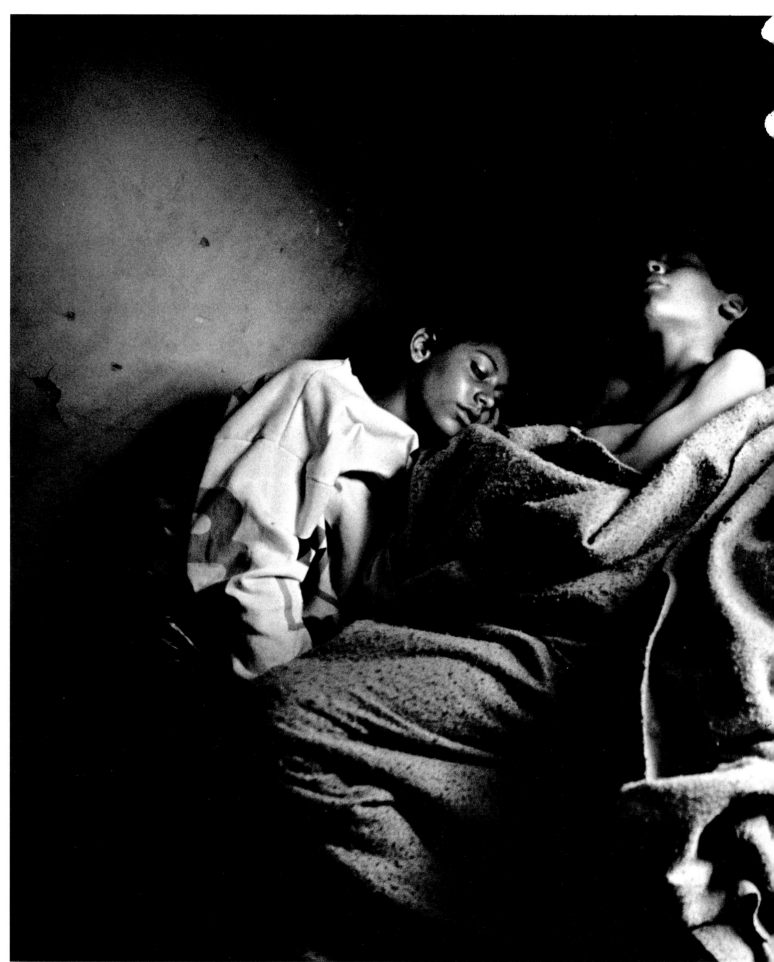

CHICAGO, ILLINOIS, 1985

Three of Leopoldo and Iris' nine children. Leopoldo, who lost four fingers on his right hand in an industrial accident, cannot find a job. The family of 14 gets by on $500 a month in food stamps and $700 in welfare, more than half of which goes to pay rent on their four-room apartment. The children work at street fairs to bring in extra cash.

Every school day 2,478 teenagers drop out. U.S. spending on elementary and secondary education, as a percentage of our Gross Domestic Product, ranks 14th among 16 nations studied—behind Austria, Japan, Canada, and Italy.

BRONX, NEW YORK, 1989

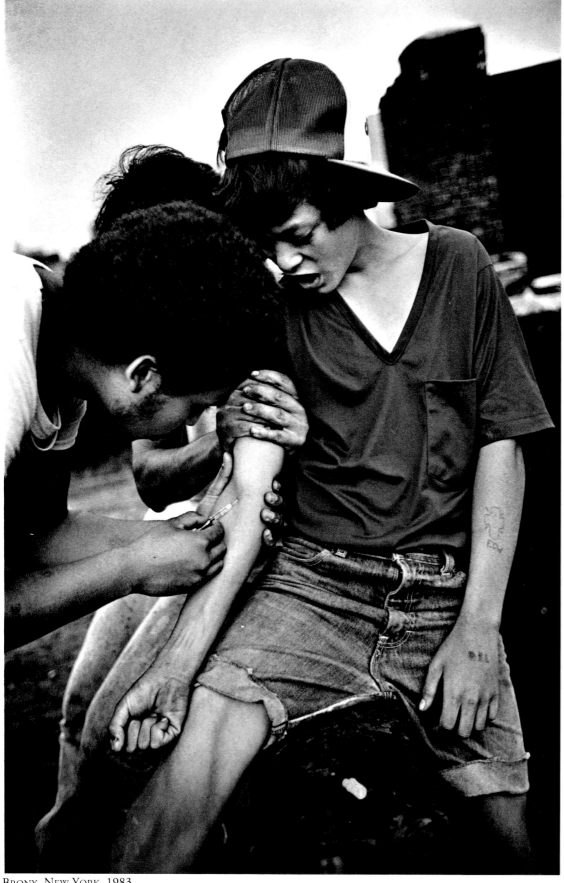

BRONX, NEW YORK, 1983

BROOKLYN, NEW YORK, 1988

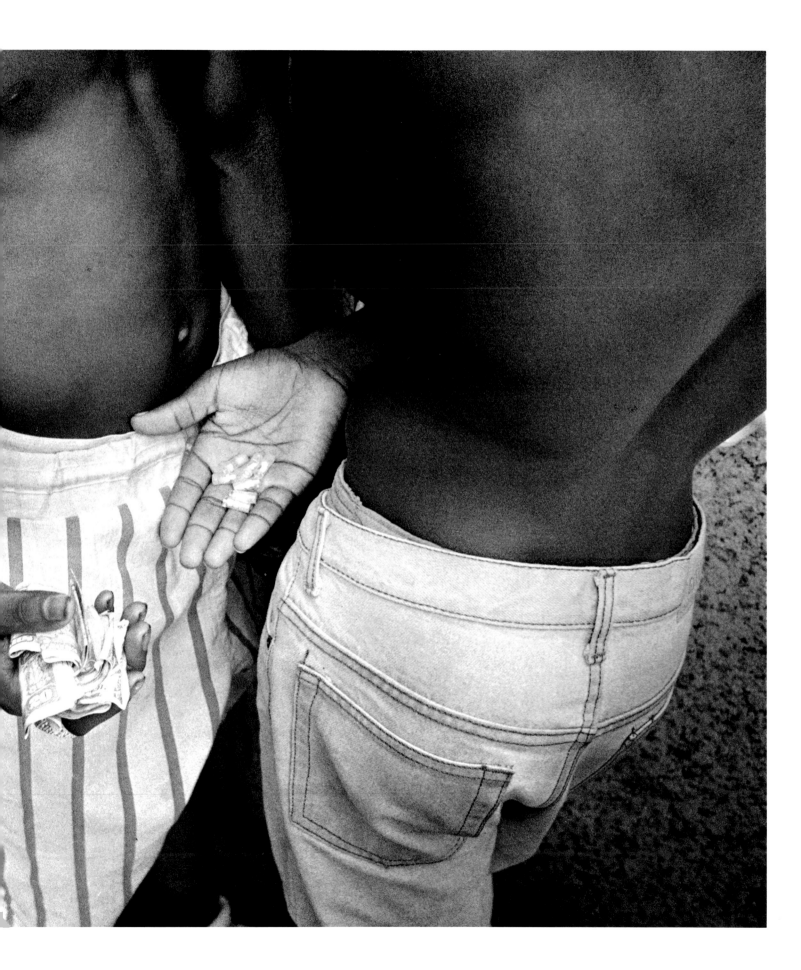

CINCINNATI, OHIO, 1985

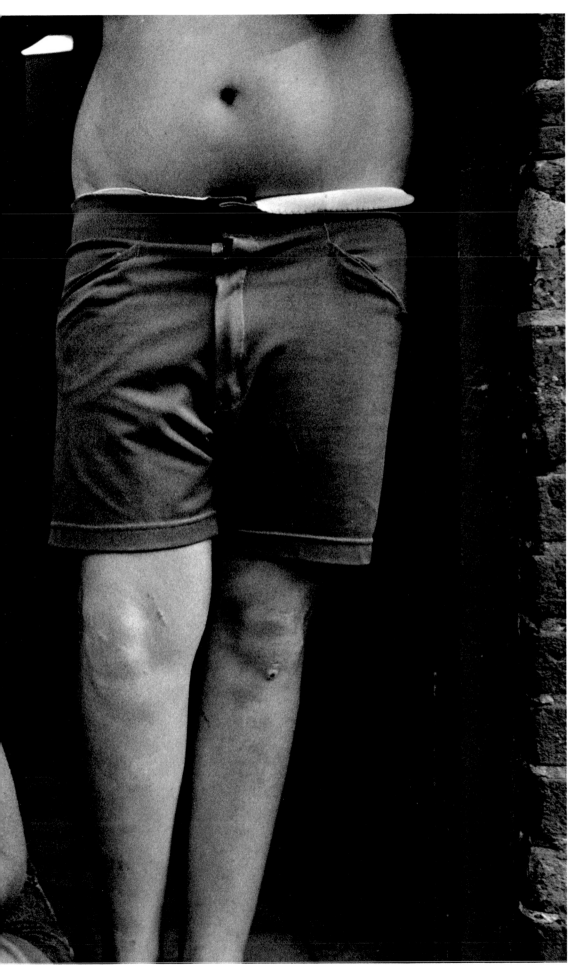

Every day up to 2 million children are left alone while their parents work. Care for one child costs almost half of the income of a parent working full time, year round at the minimum wage.

Every day 105 American babies die before reaching their first birthday.

CHICAGO, ILLINOIS, 1985

VENICE, CALIFORNIA, 1985

Each night, 40 to 100 people sleep in the pews and on the floors of the Bible Tabernacle Church. "It affects the children more than anything," one woman says. "Sleeping on the floor breaks you down, and you start getting sick."

BUCKS COUNTY, PENNSYLVANIA, 1987

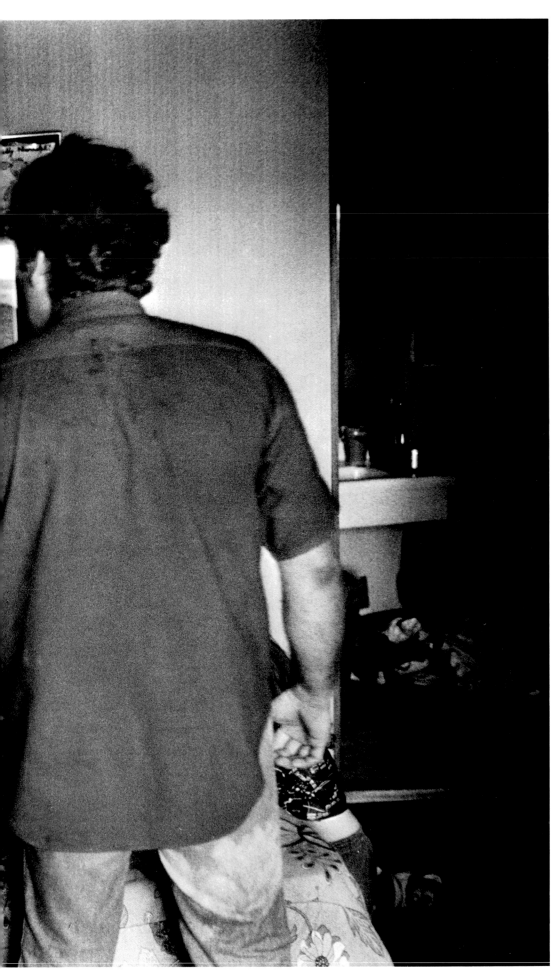

Every day thousands of women are victims of domestic violence. Some flee their homes and, with their children, join the ranks of the homeless.

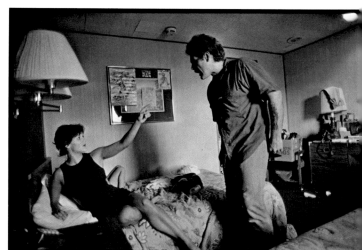

BUCKS COUNTY, PENNSYLVANIA, 1987

HARTFORD, CONNECTICUT, 1985

Every school day thousands of eligible children are denied meals through the school lunch program because of budget cuts made during the 1980s.

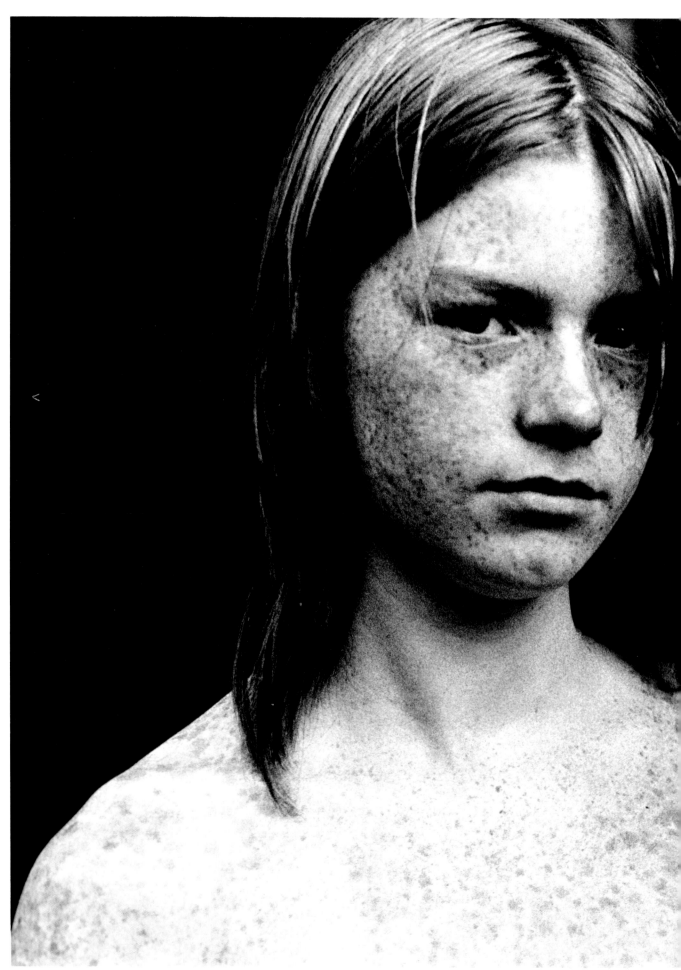

Cincinnati, Ohio, 1985

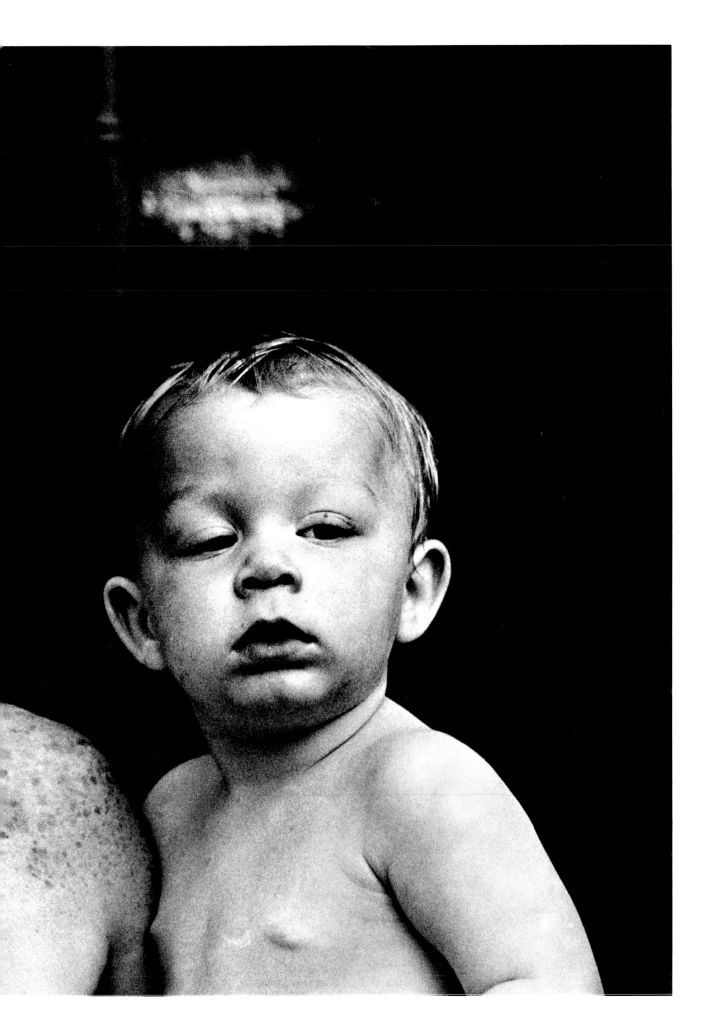

Gwendolyn, 20, cooks for 13 people, including her five children. "Sometimes I get tired," she says.

PHILADELPHIA, PENNSYLVANIA, 1985

Juan and Sylvia purchased a lot in a suburban sub-development, hoping to escape the drugs and violence of the inner city. After moving in, they discovered the water and sewage lines the developer had promised them would not be put in. The family lives without running water and is forced to bathe in a metal tub and use an outhouse. They joined with other families to form EPISO, a community organization that registered more than 28,000 voters and raised the water issue to local and state governments. Water and sewage lines are now being constructed.

EL PASO, TEXAS, 1988

EL PASO, TEXAS, 1988

EL PASO, TEXAS, 1985

El Paso, Texas, 1988

Because they hope to attend college, Bruce, David, and Willie study by kerosene lamp, the only light available to them. Their house—built by their father—has neither water nor electricity.

Toni and her six children fled their apartment when her husband beat her. Through a program to help the homeless, and after a year of searching, Toni found an apartment she could afford. Overleaf: When she and her children were homeless they lived in two rooms in the Brooklyn Arms Hotel which had no kitchen and no table at which to eat; instead they ate on the floor or sitting on their beds. The family was unable to bathe regularly since, for months at a time, their bathtub and toilet were stopped up. The children were so embarrassed by their uncleanliness that they frequently missed school.

BROOKLYN, NEW YORK, 1989

BROOKLYN, NEW YORK, 1987

Every day 2,989 children see their parents divorced. One-quarter of the divorced mothers with court orders for child support in 1985 received nothing.

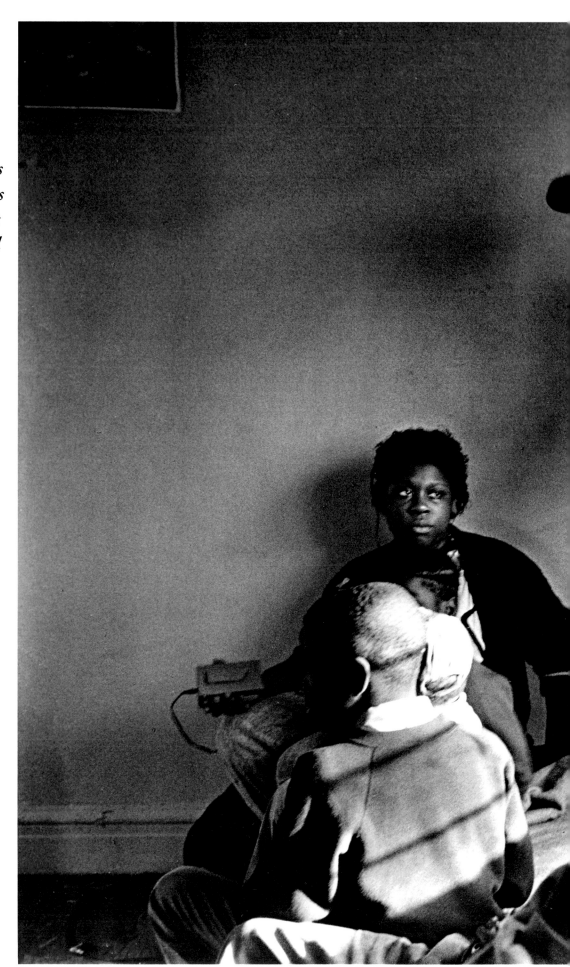

BROOKLYN, NEW YORK, 1988

The jailers of this 13-year-old first-time offender consider him an escape risk. Therefore, he must wear leg shackles every time he walks from his minimum-security cottage to class.

DENVER, COLORADO, 1984

73

PHILADELPHIA, PENNSYLVANIA, 1985

CINCINNATI, OHIO, 1985

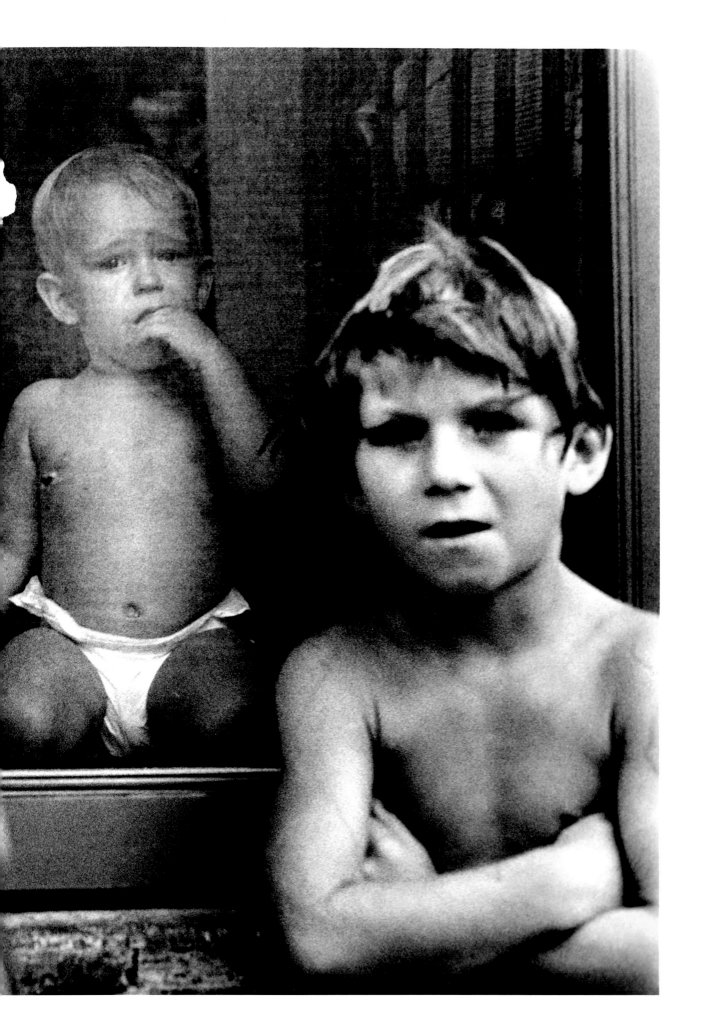

Every day in 3.4 million families with children, at least one adult goes to work, yet these families are still poor.

SHELDON, SOUTH CAROLINA, 1985

Alejandro waded across the Rio Grande when he was 14. He is now a citizen and lives with his wife, Estella, and their seven children in a trailer that's just a stone's throw from the Mexican border. He earns $3.25 an hour as a farm laborer.

EL PASO, TEXAS, 1988

Max kisses his sister Vanessa in the hallway outside their room in the Holland Hotel. Since the rooms are so small, many activities take place in the hallways, giving the place a turn of the century tenament atmosphere. Max, like many poor youngsters, provides child care for his sister.

New York City, 1987

CINCINNATI, OHIO, 1985

In this, the wealthiest nation on earth, one child in five is poor. And for certain groups of children conditions are even worse. More than half of all children in families headed by women, nearly half of all black children, and one-third of all children in young families are poor.

In fact, a child in this country is almost twice as likely to be poor as an adult. A child in a female-headed family is almost five times as likely to be poor as an elderly person.

The Children's Defense Fund believes that permitting more than 12 million of our children to live in poverty when we have the means to prevent it is un-American. There is no economic, social, or political excuse for allowing the needless suffering of children in this land of tremendous affluence.

It simply is wrong. And it is economically and socially dangerous.

Make no mistake. The nation *is* consciously sacrificing children. Each year in the United States some 10,000 children die from the effects of poverty. Poverty not only kills, it also drains children's bodies and spirits. Inadequate nutrition, untreated infections, uncorrected vision problems, lead poisoning — they all sap basic health and energy for learning. Unsafe child care, inferior schools, and dispirited and drug-infested neighborhoods kill ambition, self-confidence, and hope. Untold human potential is lost when children fall behind in school, drop out, get in trouble with the law, or have babies before they are ready to become parents. Untold dreams dry up.

Even if this country, rich in fiscal and intellectual resources (and in idealistic pretenses), continues to ignore its moral responsibility to children, basic dollars-and-cents logic should convince every American to care about child poverty. It is eroding our community fabric and threatening our competitiveness in the world marketplace. As the ranks of the elderly swell and the birth rate remains low, the proportion of Americans who are children now but soon will enter the job market is shrinking. Increasingly, these new workers will need to have the health, nutritional, educational, and other foundations that will enable them to compete in a technology-based work force, form strong families, and pay for the social programs that support older and younger Americans.

The United States *can* eliminate the terrible human and economic waste of child poverty if we choose to fight it rather than ignore it. We lack nothing but *will* and a sense of urgency.

The Children's Defense Fund joined with our good friend Steve Shames and with Aperture Foundation to produce this book because we believe that Americans from every walk of life can discover that will if they face child poverty directly and feel its toll through children's eyes.

America must *see, hear,* and *feel* the mounting cost of neglecting and abandoning millions of our children. We must ask these questions over and over again, in countless ways and places:

◆Is it acceptable that children are the poorest Americans in the wealthiest nation on earth?

◆Do we believe that the world's leading military power lacks the capacity to rank first rather than nineteenth in keeping its infants alive, and first rather than forty-ninth (behind the overall rates of such countries as Albania and Botswana) in immunizing its nonwhite infants against polio?

◆Does it offend our national pride that the United States is not one of 70 nations that provide medical care to all pregnant women? Not one of the 63 nations that provide a family allowance to mothers and their children? Not one of 17 industrialized nations that provide parental leave at childbirth, or when children are ill? And not one among the many industrialized nations with a safe, affordable child care system for employed parents?

◆Are we as a people good stewards of the future? Are we preparing now for a competitive future U.S. work force when our children know less geography than children in Iran, less mathematics than children in Japan, and less science than children in Spain?

◆How long can we tolerate the hypocrisy of national, state, and local leaders on both sides of the political aisle who mouth family values and wax eloquent about new health and education goals backed neither by sound proposed policies, investments, and strategies, nor by timetables?

Look into the eyes of the children in Steve's photographs. Feel through their eyes the threatening, hope-draining world around them. Imagine the pain of a hungry stomach, an untreated ear infection, or the discomfort and shame of sleeping every night in the back seat of a cold car or in a noisy and dangerous shelter.

Let what you see disturb you. Let it disturb you so much that it prompts you to act.

Your action can, and should, come in many forms:

◆**Inform yourself** about the status of children in your community and state, and in this nation. You can learn about the plight of American children — and steps you can take to improve children's well-being — through a variety of CDF publications. You also can visit local programs that serve low-income children and witness directly the effects of their poverty.

◆**Speak out for children.** Inform others and use every possible forum (including clubs, community groups, religious organizations, candidate forums, and letters to the editor) to help build a constituency of support for children.

◆**Accept the challenge** — and the adult responsibility —

Continued on next page

*E*very day
1,849 children
are abused or
neglected. Three
of them die.

ORANGE COUNTY, CALIFORNIA, 1984

to do something concrete to help children. You can be a child's mentor or tutor. You can volunteer at an after-school program or at a neighborhood school. You can become a foster parent or volunteer to help "boarder babies" at a local hospital. You don't have to do something grand. Just *care.*

◆**Be a role model** for children in your family and community. Remember that children do what they see you do, not just what you tell them. We can't keep children from turning to drugs, alcohol, tobacco, or irresponsible sex if we ourselves are not good examples.

◆**Hold your leaders accountable** for their stands on children's and family issues. Ask and expect candidates and public officials to commit to specific policies and programs that protect children. Get a copy of CDF's annual report on the status of children and our Nonpartisan Congressional Voting Record showing how your U.S. senators and representative voted on key measures of importance to children. Thank them if they have supported children; ask them to do better if they have not.

◆**Register and vote.** Let your vote be a proxy for the children who cannot vote and have no political voice.

◆**Be persistent.** Never give up. Our children are too important for us to let frustration, discouragement, or occasional defeat hinder our efforts.❏

HOW TO END CHILD POVERTY IN AMERICA

Between 1964 and 1969, economic growth and governmental commitment pulled more than 6 million U. S. children out of poverty. Between 1967 and 1974 we reduced poverty among older Americans by one-half, primarily through public action. Clearly, this nation knows how to reduce poverty.

Unfortunately, economic setbacks for families with children, coupled with the high cost of child care for low-income working parents and cuts in federal programs to help the poor, have pushed up the child poverty rate almost to its 1965 level. At the same time, economic, social, and tax policy changes in the 1980s helped the wealthy and hurt the middle class and the poor.

With renewed national will and strong leadership we could reverse these trends and virtually end child poverty.

This nation could — in fact, must:

◆Invest in cost-effective programs of proven effectiveness for children. Every $1 spent on prenatal care, for example, saves society $3.38 in long-term medical costs. And $600 spent for a year of compensatory education can save $4,000 in the cost of a single repeated grade. We also know that each $1 spent on preschool education can save $4.75 because of lower costs for special education, public assistance, and crime.

◆Adopt fair tax policies that do not rob from the poor to benefit the rich. There is no justification for a system that offers tax breaks to racehorse owners while failing to provide adequate

nutrition for our poor babies.

◆Place responsible limits on defense spending and redirect resources where they are needed. We must acknowledge that the enemies inside our country — poverty, drugs, illiteracy, unemployment, despair — are just as dangerous to our way of life and our future as any external threat. Eliminating just two B-2 Stealth bombers would save enough money to provide Chapter 1 remedial education services for an additional 2.7 million children.

◆Stop the perverse federal investment in fraud and waste that drains public resources from those who need help most and lines the pockets of amoral opportunists.❏

ABOUT THE CHILDREN'S DEFENSE FUND

The Children's Defense Fund (CDF) is a nonprofit research, public education, and advocacy organization that exists to provide a strong and effective voice for all the children of America, who cannot vote, lobby, or speak out for themselves. We pay particular attention to the needs of poor, minority, and disabled children. Our goal is to educate the nation about the needs of children and encourage preventive investment in children before they get sick, drop out of school, suffer family breakdown, or get into trouble.

CDF is a unique organization, focusing on programs and policies affecting large numbers of children rather than on helping families case-by-case. Our staff includes specialists in health, education, child poverty, child welfare, mental health, child care and development, adolescent pregnancy prevention, and youth employment. CDF gathers data and disseminates information on key issues affecting children. We monitor the development and implementation of federal and state policies. We provide information, technical assistance, and support to a network of state and local child advocates. We pursue an annual legislative agenda in the U.S. Congress and in target states, and litigate selected cases of major importance.

CDF is a national organization with roots in communities throughout America. Although our national headquarters is in Washington, D.C., we reach out to towns and cities across the country to monitor the effects of changes in national and state policies, to ensure their effective implementation, and to assist people and organizations concerned with helping children. CDF maintains state offices in Minnesota, Ohio, and Texas, and local offices in Marlboro County, South Carolina, and the District of Columbia. CDF also has developed cooperative projects in coalition with groups in many states.

CDF is supported by foundations, corporations, and individual donations. We accept no government funds.❏

MARIAN WRIGHT EDELMAN is president and founder of the Children's Defense Fund, 122 C St., N.W., Washington, D.C. 20001.

CHICAGO, ILLINOIS, 1985

Publication of this work was made possible, in part, by the Children's Defense Fund. Aperture gratefully acknowledges their support.

Composition By Adams Graphics, Philadelphia, Pennsylvania.
Printed by South China Printing Co. (1988) Ltd. in Hong Kong.

Library of Congress Catalog Number: 90-084833
Paperback ISBN: 0-89381-475-x
Hardcover ISBN: 0-89381-468-7

Aperture, Inc. publishes a periodical, books, and portfolios of fine photography to communicate with serious photographers and creative people everywhere. A complete catalog is available upon request. Address: 20 East 23 Street, New York, New York 10010.

The staff at Aperture for *Outside the Dream: Child Poverty in America* is:
Michael E. Hoffman, Executive Director
Andrew Wilkes, Editor
Jane D. Marsching, Assistant Editor
Susannah Levy, Editorial Work-Scholar
Stevan Baron, Production Director
Linda Tarack, Production Associate

Book design by Bert L. Fox

ACKNOWLEDGMENTS

I want to thank the Alicia Patterson Foundation, Homeless in America Photo Project, and the Children's Defense Fund, which provided support for this project. Without their generous assistance I would never have gotte out of the starting gate.

Special thanks to Bert Fox for his marvelous sense design and picture sequencing, for understanding my photos—even when I didn't—and for having the patience explain them to me; to Sarah Lazin, my book agent, for staying with this from the beginning; to Leslie Goldman a Julie Ades for their help conceiving and editing this work a for their support while I was on the road; to Andrew Wilke and Stevan Baron for pushing me to make this the best boo possible; to Phyllis Stoffman for doing more than her share parenting during the years I was gone; and to Josh for understanding how important this was and letting his dad take pictures when he should have been at home.

My gratitude and warmest feelings to the followin families for taking me in, feeding me, and allowing me to intrude in their lives: Holzer, Langner, Wallace, Hall, Walt Burgos, Parajas, Salais, Solares, Tubbs, Haraschak, Beck, O'Connell, Bonilla, Ellman/Semple, Ruelas, Dumont, Coburn, Del Rey, Shankle, Walters, Toler, Simpsons, Van Horn, Rosen, Ackerson/Summerall, Tavares, McManus, Moffitt, Houston, Smith, Chuck & B.J., Zornes, Romo, Augusta, Perez, Reyna, Ulloa, Espinoza, Hawkins, Gilham, Baron, Major, Williams, and Sanders.

Finally, I want to remember the following individuals and organizations for their help: Eugene Robert Michael Evans, Donna Jablonski, Janet Simons, Evelyn Ro Marjorie Brown, Cathy Trost, Helen MacMaster Coulson, Guy Cooper, Max King, Alison Morley, Steve Dietz, Sue Coliton, Steve Larson, Jim Wilson, Jim Dooley, Bob Drog Steve Gittelson, Michael Rosenblum, Bill Luster, Father Ed Roden, Maggie Martinez, Sister Pearl Caesar, Dr. Katherin Cristoffel, Sheila Gam, Maxine Greer, Larry Davis, Fred Mann, Avery Rome, Mark Geisler, Ron Figueroa, Judy Tri D. Gorton, Seymour Crayne, Maura Maye Midgett, Jon Hooper, Carol Bernson, Robert Asman, David Swanson, Jc Silvern, Linda Lipton, Walter Anderson, Linda Green, Alex Kotlowitz, Bob Mishlove, Jerrie Miglietta, Bob Post, Lois Myller, Cynthia Borg, Wendy Byrne, Claire Rosseel, Jane Greene, Sarah Eswein, Mark Godfrey, Mary Kelly, Alice Petry, Dr. Quentin Young, Dr. John Stockdill, Karen Greenslate, Ronald Carr, David Wells, Peter Howe, Derek Shearer, Nancy Mintie, Nancy Bianconi, Harry Rodgers, Martha Hartnett, Sheila Stebbins, Ethel Seiderman, Ken Lubas, Jimmie Pace, Reverend Alice Callahan, the *Philadelp Inquirer, Chicago Magazine, Newsweek, U.S. News & World Report, Los Angeles Times, New York Times Magazine,* CBS Sunday Morning, EPISO, Marillac House, Woman's Agend Bucks County Housing Group, United Steel Worker's Unic (Local 65), Uptown Coalition, Family Resource Coalition, ACES, Transitional Living Program, Lutheran Social Service Better Valley Services, Catholic Workers/Inner City Law Center, Association House, Catholic Social Services, Association of Hmong, Bible Tabernacle Church, Long Bea Shelter, House of Ruth, Legal Aid, United Way, Las Familia St. Joseph's Center, Ventura County Habitat, Traveler's Aid Institute for Children's Resources, Colorado Division for Youth, and the Salvation Army.

DATE DUE

JUL 1 0 1995			
AUG 0 2 1995			
FEB 1 9 1996			
MAY 1 7 2001			